T0209976

SEEK
HIM

J. M. Kellsey

WESTBOW
P R E S S®
A DIVISION OF THOMAS NELSON
& ZONDERVAN

WestBow Press books may be ordered through
booksellers or by contacting:

WestBow Press
A Division of Thomas Nelson & Zondervan
1663 Liberty Drive
Bloomington, IN 47403
www.westbowpress.com
844-714-3454

ISBN: 978-1-6642-8617-7 (sc)
ISBN: 978-1-6642-8616-0 (e)

Library of Congress Control Number: 2022922606

Print information available on the last page.

WestBow Press rev. date: 01/31/2023

*And they heard the sound of the L*ORD
*God walking in the garden in the cool
of the day, and the man and his wife
hid themselves from the presence of
the L*ORD *God among the trees of the
garden. But the L*ORD *God called to the
man and said to him, "Where are you?"*

—GENESIS 3:8–9

*"Let not your hearts be troubled. Believe
in God; believe also in me. In my Father's
house are many rooms. If it were not
so, would I have told you that I go to
prepare a place for you? And if I go and
prepare a place for you, I will come again
and will take you to myself, that where
I am you may be also. And you know
the way to where I am going." Thomas
said to him, "L*ORD*, we do not know
where you are going. How can we know
the way?" Jesus said to him, "I am the
way, and the truth, and the life. No one
comes to the Father except through me.
If you had known me, you would have
known my Father also. From now on
you do know him and have seen him."*

—JOHN 14:1–7

In the coming pages are short devotionals designed not because they have theological depth but because we sometimes slide past the most basic of truths God designed us for relationship with him. Our fullest life comes when we take the aid of Christ and walk with God. This journey starts simply: acknowledge God by seeking him. Each scripture pulled from different places in the Bible reminds us to slow down to that place where we embrace our Heavenly Father who loves us and invites us to find a greater life in his ways rather than our own.

May I, may you, and may we *seek him*.

ACTS 17:22–31

That they should seek God, and perhaps feel their way toward him and find him. (vs 27)

$\mathcal{H}$ow COMPELLING THE WORDS "FOR in him we live and move and have our being (vs 28)." Feel the weight and depth of that statement. We all exist through him. Every second that our breath rises and falls comes from him. He is not far from us; more boldly, every moment of our life can be traced back to his provision. Considering the grace of God to be ever providing for us, it seems wise that we, within our breaths, pause our tirade of thoughts, plans, and desires to focus solely on him. We discover what joys come when we align ourselves with him. Process it again. "In him we live and move and have our being." *Seek him.* He chose to be near you. Are you choosing to be near him?

PSALM 27

One thing have I asked of the Lᴏʀᴅ, that I will seek after: that I may dwell in the house of the Lᴏʀᴅ all the days of my life. (vs 4)

𝒮ʜᴀᴍᴇ ᴀɴᴅ ꜰᴇᴀʀ ᴄᴀɴ ᴏꜰᴛᴇɴ be used to motivate us away from God. However, we see from David that even in dark circumstances, doubting and cowering have no place. In fact, in dark circumstances cry out boldly for intimacy. David asks to be invited into God's home and look upon his face. Things may try to make this seem too bold, but hear this: even if your own father and mother have forsaken you, God will not. The Lord will take me in (vs 10). No one has loved you more, hoped for you more, forgiven you more, rejoiced over you more, and longed for you more. *Seek him.* Wait with active expectancy no matter the circumstances, knowing God's face is looking down in love.

ISAIAH 55:6–11

*Seek the L*ORD *while he may be found; call upon him while he is near. (vs 6)*

*G*OD PROMISES FREE PARDON. HE promises mercy. The chasm between the ultimate being in the universe and you was worth his effort. Without question, though he belongs above, God is heavenly. His promise isn't to come low and stay low but to raise up. He desires to bring us into a kingdom not of this world. To be blessed by his presence and to live in his kingdom, we must move past our thoughts and ways. His word will prosper, but we will only recognize it if we have sought his ways. Asking him for pardon is the beginning of a journey that takes us past the ways we know. *Seek him.* Come, ask, listen, and learn from him.

2 CHRONICLES 34

For in the eighth year of his reign, while he was yet a boy, he began to seek the God of David his father. (vs 3)

WHAT INSPIRED JOSIAH TO RETURN to the Lord is not mentioned, but he is diligent to remove idolatry from the land. Later when Josiah hears the book of the Law, he is immediately struck with fear. He doesn't believe all the altars, Asherah poles and cast images he has already destroyed are protection from God's wrath. Look at God's response to Josiah. Look at what God commends: Josiah's authentic heart and remorse for the people's sin. While his actions were good, they were not the depth of Josiah. Josiah's genuine fear of God carried far more significance. *Seek him.* Build a relationship not based on what you do for him but on knowing him.

PSALM 53

God looks down from heaven on the children of man to see if there are any who understand, who seek after God. (vs 2)

$\mathcal{T}$HIS PSALM IS A HUMBLE reckoning. A challenge to those of us who often believe ourselves wise but live like the fool. Certainly the world is full of arrogant people confessing no God. However, it is also dangerous to be ignorant living like we won't be held to account. We move about acting confident, believing that makes us wise. We forget about God's position and focus only on our worldly aims. All the while, God watches from above, waiting for the truly wise. The one who looks up for help. Those who hold true understanding will call out to God. If we want to elevate ourselves, we must start by asking God to guide our ways. *Seek him.* Look up to God, and ask for understanding.

PSALM 63:1–5

O God, you are my God; earnestly I seek you. (vs 1)

*D*AVID WROTE THIS PSALM WHILE in the wilderness. The environment he was surrounded by caused him to cry out with hunger to the Lord. He reminisced over the glory of God he had seen and rejoiced in God's goodness still present with him. The environment had changed, but David didn't let it slow his worship. We can find our environments wearying us or inspiring us. However, God is our God in all places. Always, he is worthy of praise. *Always.* His love is better than life. Our souls need to delight in him. Spending time on him nourishes our spirits. Whether the environment around us is a prison or a palace, our souls can come to a feast when we come with earnest, humbly and diligently looking to revere God. *Seek him.* Rejoice in who God is.

DEUTERONOMY 4:21–31

*But if from there you seek the L*ORD *your God, you will find Him if you look for Him with all your heart and with all your soul. (vs 29)*

𝒫LEASE DON'T MISUNDERSTAND THIS. THE God who built the universe in all its intricacy designed for you to be centered on him, and when you aren't, he knows you are missing your best life. The promise that you must look with all your heart and soul isn't an arrogant demand made by an egocentric God but the dosage necessary for healing medicine to revive your life. Why focus on things that cannot see, hear, eat, or smell? Why spark his jealousy when infinite life is waiting? Why be satisfied by a life that can't bring sincere joy. *Seek him.* Live. Live abundantly (John 10:10).

PSALM 34:8–14

*Those who seek the L*ORD *lack no good thing. (vs 10)*

*D*AVID'S LIFE ENDED WITH WEALTH. However, when you read scripture, you will not find him spouting on about material things. Rather the opposite. David's focus was on God. David speaks of interacting with the goodness of God personally, going past tradition and routine, and encouraging senses to interact with God with humility and respect. His awe of God didn't keep him distant but prompted him to humbly indulge in our Maker.

David writes this in hardship while he holds fast to the fear of the LORD. In hard places, David lingered not on what was missing but on God's goodness. Come in awe under this immense God whose desires are for you. Do not trust the world's hollow promises but the LORD who is good. God is faithful through all seasons of life. *Seek him.* Tangibly, with respect for who he is.

1 CHRONICLES 18:6, 13; 22:18-19

Now set your mind and heart to seek the
Lord your God. (vs 19)

God is with you. Rest on every side. The land is subject to the Lord and to his people (vs 18). Such amazing success after years of hardship, battle, and struggle! The retirement moment, feet up, and relax. Or less long term, kick back because it's the weekend. However, David is purposeful in victory and purposeful in rest. Devote your heart and soul to seeking the Lord your God. Too often peaceful times become idle times. Gifts sought in the season of hardship are forgotten. The reliance on God that has been found is cast aside. Dependence on God is not time or situation sensitive. Seeking God is a continual process. Battles may have created reliance, but we come to him at all times for relationship. *Seek him.* Hallmark your life with steady devotion.

1 CHRONICLES 28:1–10

If you seek him, he will be found by you.
(vs 9)

$\mathcal{G}$OD IS NOT DECEIVED OR pleased by Sunday devotion. He is not looking for a routine. God is genuine and authentic. He would rather have honest rage than false submission. He has no need for hollow words and false devotion. He knows what you love; he knows where your mind wanders. Please don't be confused. God gifted us with imaginations and creativity. It is his desire for hearts and minds to flourish. He is where flourishing starts. He gifted you with purpose. Look at yourself; question your heart and mind. Expose yourself. You may surprise yourself, but you will not surprise God. Give him your heart and mind daily, for as your thoughts grow day by day, let God be in them. The truth is he already knows them. *Seek him.* How able could you be, how content could you be, with wholehearted devotion and a willing mind?

GENESIS 5:21–24; HEBREWS 11:1–3; 5–6

And without faith it is impossible to please God, because anyone who comes to him must believe that he exists and that he rewards those who earnestly seek him. (vs 6)

*E*NOCH LIVED FOR OVER THREE hundred years, but we know little about him. We do not know where he lived, who he married, places he traveled, or lessons he learned. We do not know if he was shy, brave, talented, or creative. Enoch is a mystery. Yet his name is mentioned among the great titans of faith with an amazing commendation: he pleased God.

Enoch walked with God; he put the pursuit of relationship with God as a reward worth the effort. Knowing God exists isn't enough. He is God of the universe who sacrificed his Son so that you might be named his child. Be his child; it will please him. *Seek him*. Do it as you walk about your day as your life moves; move with God.

2 CHRONICLES 7:11–16

If my people who are called by my name humble themselves, and pray and seek my face and turn from their wicked ways, then I will hear from heaven and will forgive their sin and heal their land. (vs 14)

*L*ONG AGO, THE TEMPLE WAS a place, a journey. It was designed to highlight the living God to all nations, but true sacrifice to God was never geographical or material. God's eyes look for humble hearts. He doesn't despise a broken heart (Psalm 51:17). Rather that is the greatest of sacrifices. There is no place God will not go to reach a humble heart. Be moved to humble yourself, seek his face, and turn from wicked ways. God's call does require change. There was a place filled with gold, silver, bronze, precious jewels, fine linens, and the sweetest aromas, but it was not the temple God desired; you are. *Seek him.* You are the temple, the place his eyes and heart will always be.

EXODUS 33:1–17

Everyone who sought the LORD would go out to the tent of meeting. (vs 7)

𝑀OSES GIVES A POWERFUL REMINDER in this passage that success without God is no success at all. The LORD promised to bring the people of Israel to the Promised Land. The LORD would fulfill the promise, providing a rich, beautiful land free of outsiders. To some, this proposal would seem a fine opportunity. Moses though, who spent time in the tent of meeting and had obeyed God to bring Israel up to this point, saw the emptiness of this proposal.

Living without God's presence is not living at all. Better to be in the desert with God than in paradise without him. For what does it profit a man to gain the whole world and forfeit his soul (Mark 8:36)? *Seek him.* The greatest joys are only found when we remain in his presence.

2 CHRONICLES 20:1–30

Then Jehoshaphat was afraid and set his face to seek the LORD, and proclaimed a fast throughout all Judah. And Judah assembled to seek help from the LORD; from all the cities of Judah they came to seek the LORD. (vs 3–4)

$\mathcal{T}$HEY HUMBLED THEMSELVES. SEEKING CAN only be authentically pursued from an attitude of humility, of purposefully placing oneself in a low position. To underscore their need and highlight their dependence on God, they fasted. "For we are powerless against this great horde...our eyes are on you (vs 12)."

In seasons of weakness, it can feel illogical to further expose ourselves and to deprive ourselves. As people of faith, it is actually our secret weapon. In faith, humility paired with a choice to deny self becomes a powerful physical positioning of dependence mirroring what our heart and spirit are claiming. *Seek him.* Humble yourselves, therefore, under the mighty hand of God so that at the proper time he may exalt you (1 Peter 5:6).

2 CHRONICLES 17:3-6; 18:4-6, 31;
19:1-3, 7-9; 20:35-37

Set your heart to seek God.
(2 Chronicles 19:3)

𝒢OD IS IMMENSE AND AMAZING. His capacity to utilize all his attributes cohesively, in every moment, is part of his greatness. We often break God down, seeing him through pieces of his attributes. We highlight his love, mercy, and grace. Those are brilliant parts of him, but it can cause us to take liberties. Jehoshaphat took such liberties. While he had a heart for God and knew the value of seeking him, Jehoshaphat chose to be led by the king of Israel, ignoring the messages of God.

The fear of God is the beginning of wisdom because treating God fearfully places him above all other voices. If we are following others and trusting his love to forgive us, our heart is settled in a dangerous place. *Seek him.* Lean into trusting all of him all the time.

JEREMIAH 29:4–14

You will seek me and find me, when you seek me with all your heart. (vs 13)

$\mathcal{J}$EREMIAH 29:11 IS A LOVELY, popularly quoted scripture full of rich promise. Sometimes we forget the original context. The promise was written to the Israelites who were spending seventy years in exile as a consequence to sin. The rich promise we love is a reminder to embrace difficult situations caused by ourselves. When we have sinned and the Lord in his wisdom uses discipline, embrace it. Trust God in the places you don't want to be. Sacrifice your plans, accepting God for his plans. When you cry out to the God of this universe, he will hear you and listen. When you seek him with your whole heart, you will find him. How tremendous in our failure that he gives that promise. *Seek him.*

The God of the universe is waiting to interact with you, for the purpose of doing marvelous things with your life!

PSALM 78:32–39

They sought him; they repented and sought
God earnestly. (vs 34)

*L*ET'S BE REAL. WE CAN'T constantly live in alignment with God. As children of God, our flesh will lose the war, but it wins some battles. This scripture is a warning to avoid the turbulent and painful path the Israelites took. God didn't intend walking with him to be a tug-of-war match where great energy is exerted but never forward momentum. We are not yoyos; we are meant to stand firm on the rock. Remember when he redeemed you. Keep reminders of his goodness and provision to hold you steady. Avoid complacency. Stand on the solid rock. *Seek him.* Take in the truths of the past and dwell on them till your heart is stirred to awe and your lips yearn to praise!

2 CHRONICLES 11:13-17

*Those who had set their hearts to seek the
L*ORD* God of Israel came after them from all
the tribes of Israel to Jerusalem to sacrifice
to the L*ORD*, the God of their fathers. (vs 16)*

*T*HE PINNACLE OF SEEKING GOD is a heart issue. The place
to start, and the only way to create solid forward
movement, is dedicating the heart. While this
action is completely personal and private, it also,
if earnest, will transition into community. When
locked into seeking God, there is a tug to seek him
with others. Thankfully it's not necessary to trek to
Jerusalem. But community will mean self-sacrifice,
giving, and serving.

In finding God, there should be delight and challenge
that comes from putting energy into uniting with
others whose hearts are also seeking him. *Seek him.* It
becomes a beautiful thing when we direct our hearts
and bring alignment as a community to him.

2 CHRONICLES 14:2–7, 11–12

We have sought him, and he has given us peace on every side. (vs 7)

*A*sa CHOSE TO CONSISTENTLY AND diligently seek God in many different seasons. It's clear that he had integrity as a leader and truly sought God because the land experienced a time of rest. When this rest came to an end with war, what did Asa do? Asa cried out to God. He didn't demand support based on his own merits. He looked to the always faithful God. Notice there is no reference to Asa sinning and the Cushite army coming as a consequence.

This world brings unexpected trials and hardships. Asa shows a wise example of what to do in those situations. Trust God. Acknowledge the Almighty God, and rely on him. *Seek him.* Make it a pattern—the one consistent thing in a world that is always shifting.

2 CHRONICLES 15:10-15

They entered into a covenant to seek the
LORD. (vs 12)

$\mathcal{A}$N OATH SO COMMITTED THOSE of the nation who refuse will be put to death? In our world of "you do you and I'll do me," it's almost unfathomable. However we must understand this from its cultural context. They were the chosen people of God. They had wholehearted praise; they were eagerly seeking God. The community is authentic and motivated by their past. They trusted God and chose to live set apart among the nations. They were God's chosen people, but it wasn't just a name they wanted their actions to line up with the honor they were given. They were vibrant, joyful, and committed to God. Be confident with the foundation you are standing on. Let him make you bold. A fire for God can't grow in a complacent heart or community. *Seek him.* Be earnest. Wholly desire him.

AMOS 5:4–15

Seek the Lord and live. (vs 6)

*S*OMETIMES THE MOST MUNDANE, OBVIOUS, things must be said. When seeking God, also seek goodness. Consider your actions, financial choices, and words. Are you seeking good? Have you responded to the poor? Are you taken in by deceivers and rejoicing with liars? Interestingly the wise aren't called to great campaigns fighting down the system. However, they are to stay clear of those who seek evil, avoiding many words. We far too often speak with noble goals but disastrous results. Remain faithful by seeking good and staying quiet when evil calls for the joy of fruitless banter. Don't cheer with the crowd. Check your path. "What does the Lord require of you but to do justice, to love kindness, and to walk humbly with your God (Micah 6:8)?" *Seek him.* Delight in justice and goodness.

2 CHRONICLES 30:6–11, 18–21

*May the good L*ORD *pardon everyone who sets his heart to seek God. (vs 18–19)*

ᴛHERE ARE MOMENTS AND SEASONS in which every intention is good, the desire for obedience is authentic, but we fail. Despite great planning and setup, we fall short. Perhaps we have given time and resources and made sacrifices yet with all our effort to be faithful were not. The striving in earnest for holy, righteous behavior crumbled and expectations were not met. "The LORD your God is gracious and merciful and will not turn away his face from you, if you return to him (vs 9)." That promise and his character are true. He longs to forgive you and heal you. Fall upon the mercy and grace of God. Trust that by turning to him, after falling short, he knows the heart and gives redemption. *Seek him.* Look to him for pardon.

MATTHEW 6:25–34

But seek first the kingdom of God and his
righteousness, and all these things will be
added to you. (vs 33)

$\mathcal{W}$E CAN BE MASTER MANIPULATORS often fooling only ourselves. We justify our concerns, our attentions, and our exertions by calling them needs, focusing only on the physical right before our eyes. But God knows what we need, and he sees beyond the physical to the spiritual.

To conquer death, we need righteousness. God made Christ, who never sinned, to be the offering for our sin so that we could be made right with God through Christ (2 Corinthians 5:21). The Amplified Bible adds that we are placed in a right relationship with him by his gracious lovingkindness. Put your real need first. *Seek him.* Lean into his gracious lovingkindness, and let him add to you.

PSALM 69:6–18, 30–33

You who seek God, let your hearts revive.
For the LORD hears the needy and does not
despise His own people who are prisoners.
(vs 32–33)

$\mathcal{T}$HIS IS SUCH A HEAVY psalm. It's full of absolute despair and reproach, a coupling of drowning and scorn by the community that could provide aid. There is no friendship here; already feeling humbled, the community leans in to grow humiliation. From this lonely place is a hidden triumph. "But as for me, my prayer is to you, O LORD. At an acceptable time, O God, in the abundance of your steadfast love answer me in your saving faithfulness. Deliver me from sinking in the mire; let me be delivered from my enemies and from the deep waters. Let not the flood sweep over me, or the deep swallow me up, or the pit close its mouth over me (vs 13–15)." *Seek him.* Wait in confidence, knowing his response is sure.

DANIEL 6:1–22; 9:1–3

So I gave my attention to the Lord God to seek Him by prayer and supplications, with fasting, sackcloth and ashes. (Daniel 9:3)

𝒟ANIEL HAD A HABIT THAT he put his time into daily for a very long time. In different places, scripture shows Daniel reached out to God in despair with pleas, confessions in faith, and thanksgiving. He used prayer to connect with God not simply daily but repeatedly within the day. It is the practice of seeking God that allowed him to stand firm in the face of strong persecution. Daniel knew about the document and its consequences. His plan of "attack" (what gave him the strength to enter the lions' den) was faith that his consistent pattern of connection to God was all he needed. *Seek him.* When storms arrive, let your everyday habit have you planted in a place of victory.

LAMENTATIONS 3:1–33

*The L*ORD *is good to those who wait for Him, to the soul who seeks Him. (vs 25)*

*L*AMENTING MEANS TO GIVE A passionate expression to grief. The words on these pages are harsh and sorrowful, depicting death and pain in their ugliest form as Jerusalem enters captivity—after the people hardened their hearts to God. Many prophets had been sent to encourage and warn the people, but they chose worldly pleasure over God. So God allowed the weight of their sin to come upon them.

Here in the tumult of that crushing, we find the steadfast love of God and hope. Christ died for you to be saved from judgement; it is the greatest joy of the Lord to see his children turn to him. "For he does not afflict from his heart (vs 33)." *Seek him.* There is no sin that he will not forgive when we come in lament and trust in the abundance of his steadfast love.

PSALM 119:1-10

Blessed are those who keep his testimonies,
who seek him with their whole heart. (vs 2)

𝒯HIS PASSAGE HUMS WITH ZEAL for the Lord. One living with a hunger to walk in his ways, desiring to follow God, loving his commandments, and keeping his testimonies. Yet even if one reaches the tip-top of human perfection, it will not equal godliness. His nature is a holiness all our striving and desiring can't obtain; he is set apart from us. Even though our grasping can never reach, we continue on all the same, pursuing God the Most Holy. Then in understanding, we cry, "do not utterly forsake me (vs 8)." For in that humble cry, that truth, we have fallen short. We receive the answer "I will never leave you nor forsake you" (Hebrews 13:5). *Seek him.* Love to draw near to him.

JOHN 5:30–44

*I seek not my own will but the will of him
who sent me. (vs 30)*

THIS IS A BIG "CHECK YOURSELF" scripture because it was obviously spoken to those of no faith, but our actions can often be in line with those of no faith. The first verse is stunning as Christ, the Holy Son of God, confesses to only find accomplishment with the Father. I can do nothing on my own (vs 30). Not your typical self-help line here, but oh so imperative for the authentic follower. Dependence and neediness are strongly scorned by our society, yet a sincere heart of faith is always reliant on God.

In all things, go back to the Father. Unsure of what to do with your time on earth if you're spending it well? Whose glory are you pursuing? *Seek him.* Be like Christ, who said, "I seek not my own will but the will of him who sent me."

HOSEA 5:15–6:1–6

I will return again to my place, until they
acknowledge their guilt and seek my face.
(vs 15)

*T*HESE PLACES OF RETRIBUTION IN the Bible can often come across as harsh so to clarify God is not a narcissist but we often are. Acknowledge God. Actively admit who he is, actively recognize his authority, actively express gratitude, and actively pursue him. "For I desire steadfast love and not sacrifice, the knowledge of God rather than burnt offerings (vs 6)." Hear the tenderness of these words, and be impacted. The Holy God would like to pardon our sinful souls and let us abide in his presence. *Seek him.* Press in pushing deeper to know the Lord.

HOSEA 10:12–13

For it is the time to seek the Lord, that he may come and rain righteousness upon you. (vs 12)

THESE TWO VERSES HOLD OPPOSITES: righteousness versus wickedness, love versus injustice, and seeking versus independence. We all make choices that will affect what side of these opposites we end on. However, please notice that our work is internal. To refresh ourselves, we cannot provide the seeds. God does that part, but we nurture them. Being self-dependent is a deception that leads to unrighteousness. We are talking about God. What can you bring him of value but yourself opened up, trusting that what he plants is what you need? *Seek him.* Those who seek and prepare for the Lord receive showers of righteousness that reap the fruit of unfailing love.

JOHN 14:6–7, 15–21

You will see me. Because I live, you also will live. (vs 19)

THIS SCRIPTURE DEVIATES FROM THE pattern in the other devotionals but is a promise of unity that is so important. In Christ, we have not simply a moment of redemption but more truly we enter a vow for partnership and get to do so with eyes wide open upon the one we are committing to. The Lord our God is one. He is interlaced Father, Son, and Spirit, and we can see him; we can know him. This world can't reach into the depths of this truth. Indeed, it has no time for the efforts this devotion urges. The promise to be in communion seen and seeing God. In Christ, aided by his Spirit living in you come into communion with Father God.

Seek him.

HEBREWS 7:25

He is able to save to the uttermost those who draw near to God through him, since he always lives to make intercession for them.